THE TREE TRIMMED INTO A FLAGPOLE AND OTHER POEMS

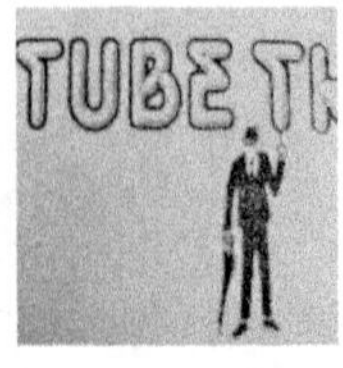

TUBE THEATRE BOOKS London

THE TREE TRIMMED INTO A FLAGPOLE AND OTHER POEMS

Acknowledgements

The Ethel Shipwreck first appeared in *Under Twenty-Five* (Jacaranda Press)

The Plastic Picker first appeared in *Overland*

First Footstep on the Moon, and *Cowgirl Nan* first appeared in *Westerly*

To the Whale first appeared in *Mum's Underground Broadsheet*

KENNETH ELLIS in these poems was boy, youth and man, a competition swimmer, a surfer, and surf lifesaver. He was a professional performer before audiences, worked in television in front of the camera and behind it.

He has lived in Australia and Britain, drawn into the sea in Australia and to the sea's side on the South Coast of England.

In the beginning were puppet shows, later newspaper and magazine journalism, but all roads can be taken back to poetry, written first of all in schooldays.

By the same author

Tube Theatre (performance)

Under the Gooseberry Fair (novel)

Punch and Judy (puppet performance)

Hidden camera, (television)

Bob Hope monologues (writer contributor)

Published by Tube Theatre

Tube Theatre Management PO Box 78603 London NW3 9AW

First edition

Tube Theatre is a trademark

 British Library Cataloguing-in-Publication Data. A catalogue record for this book is available from the British Library.

Library of Congress Cataloguing-in-Publication data has been applied for.

ISBN 978-1-7398414-0-9 hardback edition

ISBN 978-1-7398414-1-6 paperback

ISBN 978-1-7398414-2-3 e-Book

Typeset by Tube Theatre Publications

Printed and bound in Great Britain by IngramSpark

To the Esplanade at Grange

Note

These poems were written in and about Australia, Wales, and London.

I was lucky to spend much of my life living beside the Australian beaches Grange and Henley, and I hope some of the poems show the quality of those places.

My time in Wales was spent in admiration of a country that had held poetry so long and high, and wondering whether it would help me as a poet. I don’t know the outcome.

In London, I was lured by the condensed vastness and the surprising greenery.

I am grateful to the people, animals and birds who inspired my poems and became the residents of them.

August 2022

AUTHOR'S FOREWARD

THE title poem *The Tree Trimmed into a Flagpole* is one of the earliest I wrote. It was not inspired by any eco-ideology. In those days I would encounter trees damaged in such a way as to be commonplace. My inspiration came simply from recoiling at man's indifference to nature. The poem seems to have grown into an environmental hymn.

Living beside the sea, I became close to much of the wildlife, and almost felt myself at times to be one of them. *Riding a Sternum Saddle* is an example of the high profile which seagulls maintained on the beach and in the air. They seemed to insist that I noticed them.

Dogs, too, were in abundance on the sands and sometimes in the water. The poem *A Seaside Accident* merges me, my poor pet, my beachfront upbringing, and the coastal scene.

Illness and death hover at the seaside when one is living near the waves. *The Shark and the Crab* laments the suffering of my mother as I the youthful lifeguard or, properly named, 'surf lifesaver', reflected hard among the land and seascape.

A once-famous puppeteer and producer of early British television lent me his workshop near London to create my own puppet horse. The poem *Carving* also came out of the workshop.

During the Week-end of the Queen's Silver Jubilee expresses the world of the street and children's party entertainer in London.

An early poem, *The Plastic Picker*, shows how we are content with the very artificial.

Millicent (*To Millicent*) was a librarian long ago who asked me to write a poem for her. My collection in this volume contains several joke poems, like the one to Millicent, which I don't mind writing in contrast to serious plunges.

Poetry competitions are something I have avoided for a long time (*Failed Entry for a Poetry Competition on a Set Subject*).

London Doodles is an earlier collection, the title of which I thought might with its lightness work well as a balance of the heavy beauty of the great city and its sometimes intimidation of the beholder.

I tried to describe in words the mysterious ecstasy a popular song can engender, with the help of electronics. *Old Songsters* is my attempt, to recall the moods of my youth, and the effect some songs can produce. Part of the appeal is that they are time capsules: by association with the environment in which you heard them, they bring back place and people, and even can make you feel younger.

The poems are in random order, so that early poems do not always appear first. I did, however, consider each poem emotionally to stand before or after another. Some of them I had not seen for a long time, and they surprised me, for better or worse. Others, new or old, I remembered and expected the effect they had on me. It was particularly gratifying that the *London Doodles* returned the almost forgotten feelings I had for the city as a young man during my first years there.

Most of the poems are published as originally written. Revision consists of only a word or some letters here and there. However, I did complete some unfinished poems, *Two Years After My Mother's Death* and *Old Songsters,* the first written years ago, except for the last stanza, and the second much later.

The titles of my poems in general were given at the time of composition, except for a minority of them that needed clarifying, and to which I expanded rather than replaced what they were called.

A capital letter at the beginning of each line was mostly my choice: old-fashioned, some might say, as they would criticise my use of full rhymes—though not always full rhymes.

Poetry ought to be easy to remember, and rhymes help. Free verse can be a dangerous influence, especially when it is well-written. Most of *London Doodles,* however, is cast in it. Each line in a poem surely should be distinguished from prose, the composer raising it above the ordinary. Perhaps by the time my lines are read the fashion will have changed back to starting a line with capital letters and employing full rhymes. Writing new poems as I collected the old, I myself have sometimes retreated from using a capital letter to begin a line.

The poems of this collection were transcribed from original, fading typescripts, and, as the age progressed, a few from electronic copies, even composed from the start electronically, with no resort to pen and paper at all. The new way, many researchers have already expressed, will pose a problem for keepers and for collectors of original manuscripts.

I will let the reader decide which categories my poems fall into, and in which direction, if any, my work is headed. Once I have finished a poem, I do not seem to be able to turn critic and rate it. Again, I leave the job to the reader and the professional critic, if interested.

When I look at the Contents table in this book, I see a variety of combinations: craft and emotion have produced subjects and situations that were once all personal to me, but have now departed into the poems, leaving me with the memories of composition.

2022

CONTENTS

THE POEMS

RIDING A STERNUM SADDLE

RIDING a sternum saddle
Inside a seagull's chest, I heard a noise
And looked along the neck.
The wind arrived and through the nostrils of the beak
It led the frightened air come in from the world.
I laughed; suddenly the hungry beak split and
Past the wedge-shaped aperture I saw
The creaking wings hinged to the ruffled breast
And a red, webbed foot folded like a dried
Apricot heart under my one-legged bird.
Freedom declared like open handcuff rings
Waved together in the skyscape parks
Where chalky notes are taught along the sky
And comely waves assailed in arcs.

While waiting for the buxom sun
To do her naked act without the seven clouds
The pap-beaked, breast-headed men of the moon

Stamped patterns in an inch of sea on sand.
The audience of breaker boys
Applauded the thuggery of sharks
Who ate the seagulls' and the turtles' legs.
The skinny pier showed all its ribs.

I was shot out.
My place was taken by a worthy fish.
I will lay on the beach in newspaper.
Please swallow me again.

IF A RAVEN CAN SAY CHRISTMAS

IF a raven can say Christmas
Is it holier than a dove?

Stamp your name in copper,
And watch it lest it move.

For geese can march like conquerors
And cobras fear the worm.

BIG TREES LOVED BELATEDLY

THE leaves in crowds
Are anchored clouds,
Tree-tops at ease;
By journey's tubes
And dwellers' cubes
They hold, big trees.

Nature I wed
When I entered
The leaves cathedralled.
So big not seen,
Unfocussed green,
A sky installed.

Eyeball awash—
Green spray; waves dash
History. Great trees
I passed, ignored
Though blood implored—
Apologies.

THE SHARK AND THE CRAB

THE shark is steel set
In Grange beach green stone wet
At the scald of noon, wearing his emerald all,
the robes of waves,
The draped ocean broken to foam by the
anchored sand, he gapes
His sharpened shapes,
Proves
His stylus mark, the needling menace his long
bass brood
From depths to snug coves
Past the bricked, housed slope, where the
waves last sneeze, and the
Crabs fret
Genius of wet
And dry, this moving crab signs the tenancy
in mud
And now a clouded aquarium is my mother's
blood.

Doctor's white word
Says my mother is blurred,

Bed of windows sits seaward from the staring house in pain,
She my mother the host to the lodger behind the clothes chest,
The crab, evil guest.
Blame
His sideways commands, the captain of cruelty's dangerous charm
His unsteady deed.
The daily broadcast, 'O easy victory,' sing the shells;
Evil guest indeed
In trim seaweed. Crab the victor, knobbly and bent on harm,
The ruffled pines on shore gasp: 'Worse than all stings in a swarm!'

Sand beach stretched and laid,
God stitched a white broad braid,
Trimmed the uniform stern ocean's stripes fawn green and blue
To sky's horizon line; the shallows rush, and foam, and spit;
Beyond, the green wet
Hue

Of the Gulf shore slope where some swim in costumes, act the hour.
Away, out of all,
High blue moving plains, where sharks machine their gains, not one afraid
Of sea short or tall
And bid the land to stop them, and it does, I too, in a bower
Above the bones of the jetty, I in my duty's tower

Wind the siren's sigh—
Shark is embossed nearby!
On the stretched silk sea a fin makes a long skim of its try,
And I, in my tower raised from the jetty at the sun's burn
Make scenery turn
By
Siren's handle, emptying the sea of swimmers with God's gifts,
Wet costumes in blocks
Of striped colours; from the salt-bleached bones of the near jetty
The siren's skirl shocks.

Sea tiger pecks from the fresh of the shallows and shifts,
This polite shark receives the offered ocean and drifts.

'The crab cometh, O
Easy victory so,'
Cast the stranded bleats over the sea, float and sing an air
For voice and the house's unstrung lute, shadows from still windows
Blind looking in rows
Bare
Of sun, and sounds to the water come from the room's cabinets,
China deer trembling
Behind the hope's clear glass. The screen once the sea of my mother's plea and stumbling
Of my selfish young health the shark gone deep to other wrecks,
In stricken sea-facing house the crab steps his spiky treks

And slips crime from rocks
In the house robbed of locks,
The glass doored cabinet despairs as the porcelain deer feet
Tap the sea door, and to the lifesaver on the jetty tower.
The suburban deer
Bleat
Their plea for my mother to be saved by the siren's skirls
From the tower on
The jetty. Tremble the china fawns in the glass cabinet
Of the stricken room
Yet nothing comes, just cheers of youth on their waves and the shrieks of girls
And my mother sways on her vessel, while high tide rolls and furls.

THE PLASTIC PICKER

ALONG the street there are no growing things:
Lamp-posts, traffic lights and parking signs are bare;
Nothing's growing, nothing yields up anything.

But the brick-tanned hero in the suit
At the pavement record stand can live off
Asphalt as a farmer lives off earth. He's happy

Picking records, in cardboard covers glossy as apples,
Off a metal tree.

DAUGHTER OR SON

A STRAY town fetched me; persons never met
And might have been, had not I trod too soon, too late:
Old pavements new, telling gables overheard, guessed
Balcony windows, sketched wedding archways chiming, pressed
Brickwork, somewhat heaven. Corners of hope I turned,
Inventing future families. Somewhere there yearned
With custom a building, tall store of floors, a basement
Mocked me down a canal corridor, and sent
Me past a room signed *baby change*. The open door
Chided a space with judging walls and scolding floor,
The tray bare on which to lay no baby, no, none;
No flesh or bone, none: plastic spoke the mourned sad sum;

The altar tray in orange clean and worn, grand you
Daughter or son absent, but I saw you, and you
Saw me.

She or he:
'I was started to be finished.
Because started, I had to be finished.
Never said to me were the words,
'Dear or Darling.' Lips never curved
In a moon. No, never were the words
Soothed on me. I was ambushed
At the stomach slope of future,
My ambition struck down, never
Walked abroad or grew clothed ever;
Sit, stand, or lie down, promise died,
Gaze and sky stored, bright steel denied.
Never there to draw horizon
Line or summer glance, no eyes on
Someone to love or not,
My mother the enemy cut
The route to the next miracle.
My father's breath was mirror cool,

I was struck off, disqualified
By law. I willed the world, it smacked
My cheek. Yet others were allowed
To grow, slip out and fan proud.
She stretched a wire across my prospect,
And when aim made a leap I tripped.’

THE CANARY

COWARD-yellow concentrated in a cage
Sings rare reeling whirrchirrups
Better than if there were no upright rage
Of bars. Very yellow, deep, cowardly. Up
There where the ruffled birds are free

The notes are blunt; does freedom dissolve
Sharp melodies made behind the keys
Of jails? Open the cage, put him out to revolve

Around the world in the common whirlwind
And the sweetness of the song is lost
In the dust with others. Must he be pinned
To a perch to sing sweetly? His air is glossed.

Morning rose without him, his song which shone
Had gone, all gulped by yesterday's air;
The flare of daily shiny song had gone,
The bottom of his cage a rigid stare.

THE ARMADA

Approaching England 1588

EXCUSE me, gentlemen, I am of the Press—
I'll take your initial statements now.
May I move about you uninvolved? Thank you.
Ambassador—I'll take you first—I don't want your
age, nor any biographical data just yet…

'Search the flag-deck for a stormy petrel,
Ultimately we blast the River Plate;
On drums we quickly populate the shell
Grease. Crestfallen, quintessence could create
My demesne of icons in one dell,
Provided bubbles respect my bodyweight
And I sink placidly as a windless grange.
I dedicate the sick and prearrange
Obtrusive diplomacy.
Beginning with the bearing of a lozenge
Telling all the kingdoms what Spain meant,
Importunate of probable ferment,
At last the ready basking sails present
A frightful catalogue of moneys spent—
And Drake will pull his beard when he sees
assent—'

Because I'm not of this century, when I want you to stop,
I won't say enough—I'll use the word enow.
My notebook is still almost unwritten. Cabin-boy?

'The happenings will tumble blazonry,
Dooming the English lower than corsairs.
From the burning Channel to the tipped chaise
Of Elizabeth I'll mock the English airs
And see them for my children burned in steam
And petrify some heads for Spanish fairs,
And with the New World girls prepare
God to watch me toss all down the tavern stairs.
I'll kill heretic priests
And confiscate Cheap Jacks' wares.
One day, with imperial lust, I'll calibrate
Mutinous clouds myself, with a galleonful of mistresses!'

I should, old sailor, have taken shorthand down on foolscap sheets.

'Tarred bric-a-brac excels a trumpet hole
And we are acting without a curtain,
Looting along with the same shamefaced shoal,

Billowing for the scarce water's refrain
With full-length bilge-pool and stale dog-biscuit.

Rewards, stable as the slick deck-rail dodge
Barrelled in the shadowy grub-tack wheat
Like a snowstorm landing in leprous sludge,
Chording from the music sheets his symptoms minor,
Handling a baton unattached to sledge-
Hammer kindness. Be you my rightful guide?
Whether craning like an epic bridge
Will enable the sight of a creole
To frighten macaws in the green house to budge,
Is not certain. I know the boatswain
In his nightshade, and teredos in sleet
Of any colour. We are away! —knoll,
Dune and breaker, God made us certain!'

Thank you all. Best wishes to the crew.

FIRST FOOTSTEP ON THE MOON

THE moon's charge,
That marble and marshmallow glow,
Has been earthed by an expensive sneaker,
Anybody's boot—John Doe's, Joe Blow's…a ripple
sole that puts out butts
    and slips on roller-skates.

No use lying back and waiting
To float out the bedroom window,
You can't lose yourself on the moon anymore.

The moon was the poet's silver coin
But it won't spin and ring anymore.
Painters found moonlight hard to get
But now it comes as all-American quick-drying
Moonshine substitute.

That astronaut plays a hard game.

He hit the moon out of the sky.

I couldn't find it for a long time.

It’d rolled down off the altar cloth onto the linoleum.
I found it—a ping pong ball stamped MADE ON EARTH.

The nigh sky’s gone electric at a penny a unit
The Man in the Moon’s been sacked.

CARVING

FOR hours I breathed
And coughed birth dust the block of wood
Gave off, as out I eased the shape
Until a horse it stood.

So carefully
I carved; one slip, the block held tight,
Of blow or blade would have sent him
Scurrying out of sight.

He'll take his place
Hanging from a cup-hook in a row
With other puppets in a booth,
A Punch-and-Judy show.

I raised his eyes
And filed his teeth, he owes his life
To me; but I am jealous,
Knowing he will all his life

Live with laughter,
Till he is lost in nursery
Or museum; and so the wood
And paint will outlive me.

DURING THE WEEK-END OF THE QUEEN'S SILVER JUBILEE

INDOOR feelings put out shoots
Among the brick and asphalt furniture
Of the street. The road is closed, will not endure
Anything on wheels; for once, cars are unsure,
Outdone by shoes and boots.

Residents have made a living-room
Of the outdoors. Friendliness is a carpet
Under everything. The sky is low set
As a marquee roof, to touch and get
Reassurance from, not gloom.

I'm free to lie down in the road
And tuck myself in with a table cloth
From a party trestle. Like a quaint moth
The entertainer descends, with his sloth
Of a dog and his battered load.

He has a suitcase full of tricks,
And a booth of nimble painted figures;
He's a magnet, with a jolt that triggers
Human filings, and cures urchins' sniggers…
But the strained back of goodwill cricks.

Then, gradually, all virtues leak

Away. The goodwill sinks and drains like beer
From a cask dropped and split. The street is clear,
And cars barge down it, and gangs of youths leer.
    Folk keep to the pavements and are meek.

1977

TODAY

A ship
Has got
To go
To lands
Away from strife.
Shall I
Sail,
Or stay
And lose
My life?
Spies
Were stood
Against
A wall
And shot,
Their blind-
Folds burst
With fright.
War
No more
Has stopped
A day
Since
Brutus
Used his knife.

A THANK-YOU NOTE

THANK you, Mrs Saunders, for the lunch
We tucked into in a corner of the corner pub;
And thank you for shielding me, a timid cub,
From the pint-gurgling drunk who had a hunch
I was ripe for picking. Nothing but a punch
Would have removed him. I'm not the one to drub
A burbling stranger. I'd rather let him grub
In his own cant when it comes to drunch.

Thank you, also, for keeping our meeting
As brief and sharp as a poem by me;
If I am to win your continuous greeting
I must learn graceful punctuality.
For my mistimed taking of leave, I took a beating
Well deserved. Your restrictions make me free.

1978

TO MILLICENT

MY words
In view
Lie
Low
In pledge:
Can you
Espy a
Name on
Their edge?

INDOORS

SNOWFLAKES cross the windowpane
    Driven by the slanting wind
Within the limits of a frame
    Of cold landscape with clouds behind.

Because I sit in the dining-room
    At the table nearest the flue,
I can't see where the flakes come from,
    Nor where they are going to.

1969

NOISES IN THE NIGHT

A FAR night-noise, a pulse under the skin;
A near noise, like somebody breaking wind.
Is the far hum a machine serving mankind,
Or the heave of a war about to begin?
Is the near noise the house scratching its shin,
Or a burglar betrayed by a floorboard that's mined?
As a listener in bed, I'm always inclined
To fear the worst and be taken in.

The city has fiends or machines that kill you,
It's true; but as if they never existed,
I must live on, look straight ahead—the view
Must be admired. I am greatly assisted
By good luck or bad rarely being on cue,
Not able to be courted or resisted.

COWGIRL NAN

SATURDAYS, my parents on the town,
I stayed the night at Nan's. After sundown,
In the canyon of my bed sank soon
My snowy little head, alive with hold-
Ups, dazed by gunshots over film-set gold
Screened at the Odeon that afternoon.

To bring on sleep, my Nana told me stories
From the quilt's cliff edge. Mocking glories
Faked to thrill the pocket money off us young
But still to us the good old solid truth,
She said that in America in youth
She'd been a real live cowgirl—six-gun slung!

The room was dark, but for the wireless she
Left turned down to comfort little me.
Its humming, glowing dial became my fire,
The shadow of my quilt mound on the wall
Apache! creeping into camp. Nan all
In black with wind-bent hat and gun for hire

Rode through the sandhills of my dream. She tied
Her snorting horse up on the beach, outside
The shack we used on holidays, reins round
The rail we hung our striped towels on to dry.
It was a summer's night and somewhere by,

Out in the dark, the stingray sea was wound

Up tight—all night it lapped with sounds like shots
Of whisky being poured for nerves. The dots
Of distant bay side lights became the fires
Of crooks, with stubble chins, hot on the trail
Of cowgirl Nan. No one untold Nan's tale,
So as I grew, it seeped my brain's young shires

Like some old tea-cup stain that won't be budged.
No privilege of truth was it begrudged;
It pegged my thoughts out tautly as a fact.
Now, operations would not move that stain;
To cut it out would cut out half my brain.
Nan's tale supplied the night life our town lacked

And luckily, was gentlest of the lies
A man could grow up with, of bigotries
That are the guy wires holding him in drape.
Pity those brought up on lies sincere:
Never must they know they're wrong, for fear
They stab to death what's now become their shape.

A NIGHT WINDOW REVISITED

I
STREAKS of light sketch on the night
Shape of a shuttered window;
Display case of a shuttered life.
Stood outside, I, once resident
Now passer-by; the leaks of glow
Stroke my sleeve and woo my eye.

II
Not the room's, but within me light
Plays on what gleamed there, now packed
And gone; illuminated to profess
There children bloomed to height,
Confess there lovers' ground dried cracked:
Old pictures behind glass.

III
You, there, once resident,
You've not seen me, but I know
You, young man, lost inside me,
Deep in time's sediment,
Your stylish present now
My past worn out to chide me.

IV
Reunion of past and present
Would be father meeting son
I'd never known. Would lives merge,
Son accept blunders well-meant
Or ridicule me as one
Who swims the calm, avoids the surge?

V
Out of the lit-up home
Drifts the ghost of your intent,
To learn that triumph's a swish:
Not loud brass and echoing dome,
But a gust through a loosening tent.
You join me; we wish afresh.

AFTER RECOVERY

THE stinging, cold and iron grip of winter
Has squeezed me so hard that my chest's contracted.
The air's no longer smooth, it comes instead,
At every inhalation, with a splinter.
My chest was once a castaway's homestead:
Well lit, equipped, and stockaded. Hinter-
Land might glower, a savage print a
Footmark—but nothing kept my heart from bed.

One must reign the cherished to invasion.
Warm deeds can be baked in a pit that's dug
While on the run, and filled with heated boulders.
I shelter in the cove of an occasion:
An annual day, which throws its prickly rug
Of hours across my soul-surviving shoulders.

A HORSE OUT OF BOUNDS

A HORSE without a driver, cart, or load,
Had broken loose at night to use the road.
Instead of biting grass and ignoring stars,
He courted with the lights of motor cars.
Perhaps he thought the rays were strips of day,
Aimed through the darkness as a sign to play.
He capered in the beams as in a wind
And glowed in the light as he feels in wind.
He ought to have been in a roadside paddock.
I checked the fence and the gate. The padlock
Wasn't undone and nowhere about
Was a likely gap for a horse to get out.
I held one glove and slapped the other hand.
He wasn't frightened and didn't shift from a stand
He had taken to watch me come near.
His salient eyes, so dark and deep a black tear
Might have rolled, said he'd had fear,
But of the slaps and the hisses that night was the
least:
The most was of living with men when born a beast.

22 August 1966

TO THE WHALE

YOUR death's so terrible it seems just make-
believe,
An arrow-in-the-back stunt from a Robin Hood
film—
But what the harpoons buries in is real and hurts!
You sound down an ocean's canyons
Steep as the sky upside down,
And you are heavy as a planet fragment breaking
Off in space, past wild kelp jungles
With flitting fishes flowered, steam train with
forehead
Like a fortress dome, sped out through fluid
countryside
Without a toot or hiss, all too quiet,
Your eyes sticks of dynamite plugged ready to
explode
The patient boulder of your head.
Why are you gentle as an island? Why let the ships
Harpoon and anchor you, and die a blubber lump?
Your tree trunk tail could fell a funnel, flog the sea
Itself enough to hurt. Your mountain head could
make
You famous as an earthquake.

You could become the famous *thing* that drinks gulfs dry
And spits out ships like seeds.

1971

THE END

I'LL be afraid when I begin to die:
I worry even when I think of it;
But musing that the end means end of pain
Makes me a miser for the unknown gain.
Scold me like children for my fear of pain.
If sheathing a glowing sewing pin
Between the nail and live flesh of my toe
Would spare a man his hanging or a town
Invasion, I'm sure that I would yell, 'No!'
I don't boast ever to love pain, but guess
That death itself is just a weather change.

If my own death looks kind and quick and strange
I'll ask it to sit down. Perhaps I'm not
Reliable in vowing this: my age
Is twenty-three, I'm in a heated room
Surrounded by my health. We all must die,
But mothers at warm bedsides try to groom
Their children's sleep with tales based on the skies.
Men and women once smooth now are wrinkled,
Make up their minds that they will never die;
Ask their mirrors too many questions—then

Reflected wrinkles spit like lips, 'Your turn soon.'

Regard a graveyard by a circular moon.

What headstone's wriggling, though the light is strong?
Dig up the grave of someone that you knew.
What would you strike? Not him or her—a cage
Of bones, some rotten panelling. That stage
Of death's a torture of us still alive,
A disappearing trick to hurt the eyes.
But at the least call death a great relief,
Even if you don't agree with me I
Do not want to live on just the way I
Am. That would be boring and meaningless.

6 February 1969

CONFUSED CONFESSION

YOU do not have to pardon, God, for me
To qualify for absolution. I
Sin so well, repentance is a certainty.
My guilt grows fast and long like little happy
Hairs that sprout on glutton's lips and yeasty
Chins. I am ashamed and frightened of my
Deeds, contrary to the arrogance of my eye,
And I regret that you have made me free.
I'd like you to command my jaw to lock,
Or better, choose my thoughts and cast them in
The aptitudes I always try to speak—
Your son regaled well when he had a skin.

GOD

But he wore his as a true physique—
Not just an opera hat at eight o'clock.

LOVE’S ASSUMPTIONS

THE moment we married, was it chance
We joined so rightly? Does the trance
Of love apply to chosen ones all the while?
If, instead, we met when old, would the smile
Of each enhance the teeth of the other?
And if it was as useless tots, would be bother?
Believing, perhaps, we were sister and brother.

Or would we, like a sleeper in his bed,
Feel a burglar in the house though nothing said
Or done, sensing our lives were running down
Among hairdresser, bar-tender and clown—
Would all that be if we’d never met to kiss?
And if you never have you never miss?

THE ETHEL SHIPWRECK

THE Ethel shipwreck
Rusts its scurvy deck
On cheesecake sand. Prosperous barnacles
Sleep on the planks. The bread and water coast
Bends to emptiness, the sky swallows gulls
As eyesight gives them up. Curled and pretty
Shells
Lily-clean, bright and hollow, long-widowed
Of molluscs, lie on the land, dry as listening ears
in check
For cringing Ethel slipping down the rocks
Nearer the sea where sheer
Waves suck the beach opening cavernously to show
the dead.

Pity the anchor
Shifted from danger
To a crumbling cliff. Some civil men pushed
A mutual pen to crank it off the sand.
Manacled, mounted, monumental, grand,
It looked a fish-hook—and the beamy ships
Rushed
To mock, rolling in the wide horizon,
Traders of the sun clocking at ports of moneyed ken,
Bumping their fine rumps on the drumskin sea.
And on the pedestal
A polished tablet keeps: ‘The Ethel Shipwreck. All Souls Lost’.

That tablet was new
And minted as true
As Ethel was when her shipwrights were warm
With work, when she left and hurried to seas,
Shining and tight, the anchor like cross keys
Struck on her bow. But granite cliffs seem clouds
Come
Night and she glided gladly into stone,
Crumpled before the cliff was known and withered
through
The water among the grumblings of the
Stethoscopic sea which
Frightened her to land where scaly with morning
dew she starves.

The chafing ocean
And the brazen sun:
Strophe and antistrophe of strident spindrift,
A golden boulder burning solar oil:
Rigged to irritate, a viscous coil
Electrical in the spinnakered wind.
Lift
The hourglass. Rats grin on the figurehead
Like warts and eat the wooden breast as if it were a sweet;
But carved with dignity, the lady has
Her arms across the hole
And arches longingly from the crooked prow bowed on the sand.

She is in sea heat
Proud as a whole fleet,
Desiring a captain whose golden wrists
Would beckon her from her hermit crab shell
To sail away to a kittiwake dell
Through the private white fumes of the soft sea
Mists
For a very salty dogwatch affair,
His cap hung on the sun, his sextant sliding to the
treat
And flying fishy disgusted to their gills
While over the spray tilts
The anchor eager like a javelin for the green turf.

Chorus of port-holes
Grimacing like skulls
Cry bilge-water tears to shrink a captain's braid.
There smokes a floating speck and on it stands
A navy-blue man who watches the lands
Round Ethel. 'Yo-ho! my captain, yo-ho!
Staid
Sir. Come under the bridge,' the port-holes hoot.
The Ethel rests her blasted side on his sleeve
grapnels haul
His scudding heart to try to make it stay
A liver in the rocks
With lovely Ethel, hug her hips and stoke he
boiler up.

Piping a captain
Out of a mountain
Of depth is harder than charming a snake,
Not knowing that it is a cunning foot
Which gives obedience to the flute.
For ships, like fakirs, need a foot to tap.
Wake-
Making ends at the stern but shy waters
Are wealed. Ethel, do not pine after dauphins
of the Main.
Those dandy galleons, like fighting cocks
Wear steel spikes on their heels
To ride their cargoes spurring young ships'
innocence away.

THE TREE TRIMMED INTO A FLAGPOLE

THE tree trimmed into a flagpole,
Was a hideous thing;
May as well have been a hole,
When I stumbled on it in a clearing.
The animals green leaves console,
No wonder they wouldn't go near
That dead white post stark as an ear.

Though once it was a buxom tree,
Unharmed and sheltered in a spot
Of forest by friendly
Boughs which weaved a thatch—what
Of the change? If most agree
A bushy tree is better bare
The animals are rude to stare.

LOLA

for Judy Gleeson's dog never met

I

LOLA, of the photographs, but
Dog not met, I bet, white cloud pet,
Beach blessed, turned on your back, a pad
Under your paw would if I put
It close to my nose, you fair muzzle,
Like all dogs' pads, smell nice, sweet puzzle.

II

She calls you in the sea sound house,
Down some corridor whispering waves,
Or on sand, you beached in her voice,
By sea and sky's good emptiness.

To be called is to exist.
Not called, is a cool change
Like white caps on the Gulf to twist
The smooth rough from Henley to Grange.

The last call will come. The last call
Is of the day or forever.

IN MEMORY OF JUDI GLEESON

d. 7 July 2019

CURVED carved beauty, self-doubting face,
In dressing-gown or brief beach wear,
But Grange Sea grew too rough to bear
And washed away your lovely trace.
Your path is buckled, then a gap—
On you, men hone their skill to end;
Never endured, nothing would blend;
Was your child dough baked the wrong shape?
I walk into your sea glare room,
I see you crying to the phone,
A call abroad leaves you alone.
Great sun forgives late afternoon,
Waves, ambling, pat the jetty's legs;
The disc you spin—*West of the Wall*—
The other side—*The Big Hurt*—still
I play a copy and it begs
Those songs that grooves give out to flow
You from the old turntable's ease,
With that smirk of yours, sent to please.
What lies between us? I don't know,
Friendship's a word too low a sum:
We are not joined by friendship, love,
Or sex behind a sandy cove.
What are you really to me? —Um,
The worth I total up of you,

The sea air at the sight I drink
Of you, is more for you I think
Than you inhale for me, it's true.
I fear you mean much more to me
Than I to you. Was it my sleight
To raise you to the jetty's height?
Or higher still, above the sea,
Up the tower on the jetty raised
To my surf lifesaver's soothed view
Of our houses set in glue
Of the coast mosaic? I gaze
To bring back that first day you stood
And blocked the sea at my front gate.

Dear seafront ghost, I see the straight
Slim metal bolt secures my mood,
You, the beautiful long steel bolt
That pins my recall to our past—
Jetty, pools, pines, esplanade, mast—
Has rusted and slid out. I halt:
My beach has fallen from the air;
Yet waves spread thin to show your lace;
Curved carved beauty, self-doubting face,
In dressing-gown or brief beach wear.

FAILED ENTRY FOR A POETRY COMPETITION ON A SET SUBJECT

A Glass of Wine

The glass of wine glows, ready, stemmed,
To take alive; the ruby bowl
Is basin of its being, hot coal
Of personal fire. Outside, condemned,
The worlds we want less of, thresh.

The delicious, seated moment's best;
The held glass rises, tips the crest—
Wine-wave—past lips of glass and flesh;
Grape mystery floating on the tongue,
Dropping in the grotto of the soul,
Ledge by ledge, secret like a mole
Through tunnels of the veins along
The roads of longing, the final
Mountain path through clouds of mind that leads
To a magnificent view, breeds
Its own time of the year, and spinal
Cord of truth. The gentle dusk
Of wine has settled on the shape
Of every body coast and cape
And floats at last its weaving musk
Of happiness from body's cliff;
The view is beautiful and vast—

Some see it foul and vast but most
Inside themselves guard goodness that, if
Freed by wine, forms a table scene.
We cherish the still life: wine glass,
Set table and details amass
Beloved trivia. Gleams green
The bottle, and reflected bright
Shines, dealt by the painter's still-life brush
In clever oils to conjure gush,
On bottle green, of new-mown light.

Doors, window-panes, wine, table-cloths
We put about our eyes to block
The winds of wilderness that mock
And blow, dismissing us like truths
Gone into the empty night, blown
Off the face of blankness, where perch
Our hopes: domes, rock-hewn paths, a church.

Each guest is seated on his own.
The table-cloth defies the haze,
A snow-bound meadow as its spread;
The drinking glasses lit deep red.
To find warmth, faces—dear, foul—gaze.

1991

ANNIVERSARY SONG

For Australia and Britain

OF the two years we've spent
Each had its own land:
A dry flat continent,
A damp tight island.
Continent at one end,
Island at the other
World end. Seas between made
A world cover.

The continent inhabits
Southern hemisphere
Like an overweight rabbit
With one chewed ear.
The island's in the north,
Ireland's its flagon;
Its shape is, as it maps forth,
A sick dragon.

It's hard to believe that
The dragon gave
Birth to a rabbit which
Is as big as Europe.

OLD SONGSTERS

for The Mamas and the Papas

I DID not try to learn their name;
Nor what they called their songs;
Enough to hear the same
New seizing wails, diphthongs
Long, and lonely vowels,
Yearning from somewhere, sweet and strong.
Caught moods in building stairwells,
Their songs were young when I was young;
Tuned smoke, white clouds in high-blue space
Inhaled below, to smart the heart;
Their lathering notes smoothed my face,
Where I would go, where step or start,
Their strumming sketched fine
Sandhill vales and beach bird flocks
On the bare flats of my young mind.
In city hollows their word flocks
Settled then flew; and callow
Banked concrete echoed their visit,
Mountains of melody wallow
Adorned plain towns. Is it
Like the gods of old who cried

From a night cloud when over
The warm black sea and wide
Bay of my holiday hover
A surfer's unseen radio boast
Pleaded with me to hear
Waves lost against the coast
In a tune that in its time could shear
Tall sharp buildings, but moves
Now as merely vapours raised by chance
From old remembrance grooves
Rising in the indifferent air?

Draughts spilt in an idler's ear
When those four young natures came
They soon as went, left in the stare
Of fame despite it set a wound,
Bright figures of sound and fame.
They'd sold their shapes to prance—
Shapes made with skill, and powerful
To please their dancing city;
Voices made beautiful
By electricity.

Four young voices, each fresh sound
Grabbed from the sack and held to shear,
To taper, smooth, to round
By a song engineer
On the lathe of electricity.

Voices grooved, joined, stacked—
Blocks of honey-coloured pretty
Building stone, whittled, packed,
To a fine point to raise with riffs,
A spire to top a church of throats
And quake of tones cooled into cliffs,
The height a monument of notes
For voices—images apart:
More voice than bodies featured here…

It was not them but their art
That shivered me, made so clear
In voices. How much of it
Was yell prettified by electricity?
Am I deceived by the touch of it?
Yet their songs still snare me,
I am deceived and thrilled,
Knowing men gilded their looms,
And they sold singing to be milled
By engineers in sound-proof rooms.

FACES AT THE BARRIER

THE train to pull me out of view
Stood pointed; I stalked to catch it,
Looked back and glimpsed my household two
Caught as the camera would snatch it:
A smiling lady holding up a meek-faced dog.

There at the barrier she kept
Her gaze on me inside the hive,
The thread between us the crowd swept
But could not break—fond looks survive.
The smiling woman with the meek-faced dog in her arms.

The train pulled out, the bond unwound
And broke, faces safe in my head,
Pictures on the shelf of the mind,
Dear ones to float at my deathbed.
The smiling woman with the brown eyes, the little dog in her arms.

16 August 1988
6 July 1989

IN MEMORY OF FIONA SCOURFIELD

Murdered 6th March 2018

FIONA, memory charm
Of Wales half a century
Ago, you the toddler
Leaning on the settee-arm,
Parents telling you, see,
Not to climb or linger;
Red curly hair, eager
Small bud face, curly red hair,
No harm, eager bud small face.

'Sheba!'—the family's order
To their dog to behave here,
Furnished the house I trace.

Now, I in my old age, kept
Without news of you till, grudged,
I read of the crime blot
On your middle age. A swept
Hair, tender photograph lodged
With reporters shows me what
You grew into, the red hair
Still there, auburn sunlight.

Yet the harm did not dread
You, but magnified air
Around your goodness. Blight,
I have to live with you dead;
At least all your virtues
Kindly light crying fame.

THE IRON RING

PLAIN old immortal thing,
The anchored iron ring
Held in the library's side
By embracing bricks. I tied
To it my dog (now dead),
The future written, read.

Brickwork and ring abrupt
My visit interrupt,
Blank out the day by day,
Shut the present away;
Off the wall my thoughts bounce,
Events that happened once.

Tied to the ring dog blinks
And shivers, squints and winks;
Over my life she looks,
Years stacked like library books:
Events that happened once;
No lesson learned this dunce.

Over the roofs of time
Dog looks out at my prime.
Indoors, the books, bound stories;
Outside, my poor glories.
Of what does the dog show proof

By staring at local roof?

The dog proves by her stare:
What happens everywhere—
Crises, reunions, events,
Estrangements, arrangements,
Are in the end mere thought
On the face of those time fought.

Antrim Grove library London October 1991

MY TERRIER

A PUNGENT mix of black and tan; a blend
Of coat as mellow as old master's oils;
Hoarder of overlooked household spoils:
Doubloons of warmth from sun patch or log end.
Comedian with yelping yawn, you mend
Worn minutes with your wags, and daub blank toils,
And play, when you strum your chin for flea that foils,
All the music that collar and disc can lend.

Seen with a dispassionate eye, you change,
Unwrapped of pet name and chocolate box role,
As a familiar word seems strange
When stared at. Creature from another hole
Of time, our tunnels cross, and we exchange
Looks, but thoughts slip past each other by the shoal.

21 May 1978

LONDON DOODLES

St Paul's Cathedral

I

ST PAUL'S, the privileged old man from the wars;
Young buildings stand aside out of respect,
So as not to spoil his view over the roof tops.
His balding, faintly interested dome
Peers everywhere: greets a solicitor
Through a garret window, pauses to enquire
In lanes. Retired by the Thames, like
Winston Churchill in a chair, he longs for
The microphone too high to speak into—
The Post Office Tower.

II

Sharp Park Scene

HIGH railings prick the leaves,
The soaked paths sulk,
The smell everywhere of watered dust;
Puddles on the benches.
Exit slowly a nanny in tortoiseshell spectacles, with majestic pram.

A boy in a school cap chases a ball towards an unseen ice cream stall;
The till rings through the shrubs.
A sandwich eater looks up at a black cloud,
A tramp considers the breasts of a gleaming black statue.
Around the lamp posts dogs on leashes float like balloons.

III

Idea

THE striplight station sign at Stepney East,
That helps overtime workers to see to bite their fingernails
And drunkards to avoid their trouser legs when spitting
Would be a good thing
To have above my bed
So that I could feel
All the insecurity of a public place in private.

IV

Going Home

AMONG the faces bobbing in the flow,
Palomino hair, doll's eyes, and button lips,
I would not be surprised to see our own,
Because we mummers wear a common head
That fears the colours of the traffic lights.
And in the summer there's no need to watch
For rain. So the Fuhrer on the highest
Building goes unnoticed while he strings loud-
Speaker cords from roof to roof,
Primes his moustache, clears his throat
And switches on the microphone.

V

A Long Time Upstairs

A MAN who has not been downstairs
Since the night before last is shocked
By what his forehead strikes
On the last step in the hall's coloured light
From the front door's stained-glass panel.

It is only a nursery rhyme web he brushed,
Spun at human height, across the stairs, from wall to wall.

But being shut up
His imagination has grown bigger than his body,
And at the moment of touching when the feel of something

Where he expected nothing to be
Seized all time and place from his thoughts,
His imagination told him, and he believed it, that he was not in London,
And that his head had touched a two-thousand volt electric border fence

That sings like a national harp and keeps the peasants home in windy Mongolia.

VI

River Lions

IN the Embankment wall
A row of stone lion heads faces the water,
Each with a ring in its mouth,
For ships that used to tie up, I suppose.

When I on the pavement
Stop and lean on the dirty wall
To sniff and look out over the water's edge at something or nothing
The heads are below me,
Set in the wharf's sheer wall where no one can get at them,

At a level a rat would envy. In the windy sunlight
They scowl unruffled out over the splintering water,
Dignified except for the iron rings.
You can see them
Only from the river, looking back from a bridge or a barge.

I saw them after a tour of *Discovery*,
At lunchtime in my suit.
I saw them
And looked away and walked
Back up the gangplank, over the flowing grease of the Thames,
Back to the pigeons and cast-iron lamp posts
And back up the side streets to the offices.

I remember them being
So still they looked ready to move,
To let go of their rings in a row of splashes
And stretch their jaws.

Maybe bodies are joined to the heads
On the other side of the wall, and suddenly they'll
Make themselves small like cats, squeeze
Through their holes and jump on a rower going past,

Or on a flashing piece of floating paper spring.

Don't worry,
The last time their eyes were clear enough of dirt
To see was when they were new,
In honour of royal barges baroque as golden grasshoppers
Floating past.

Don’t be frightened to laugh at them,
They are a long way away
In memory, history, and distance. I am halfway
Up the first side street by now. They are
 Harmless as portly statues in the park.

But if I had to pass them
To get back to my office chair I’d
Go home to my flat instead, and if they were close enough
To touch, I’d even be afraid
To pat their stone-dead manes.

VII

Some Businessmen Seen on the Street in the Nineteen Seventies

THE businessmen that pack the blocks
Of buildings, their hands and faces
Grown out of their clothes like flowers,
Suede jowls preserved like bacon.
All that show are head and hands,
The daylight equivalent
Of tap-dancer's face and white gloves
In the spotlight—the rest's no use.
The unimportant roots are planted in suits.

If you are lucky enough to spot
An unshelled specimen beside
A swimming pool or at
The Olympic Gym you'll notice
How the head and hands are darkened
And enlarged with use.

The only live parts in this life
Are face and hands, decorated
Perhaps by thick black spectacles,
Moustache, wristwatch with expanding band, initial ring.
The dead parts, desks,

Red telephones and lacy signatures
Are the next most important things.

VIII

Businessman as Symbol: Nineteen Seventies

WHAT a noble shape the manager
With his briefcase makes of mornings,
Crossing the dumpy railway bridge,
The sky fresh dishwater colour,
The picket fence serrated black
Because of poverty of light.
Up there of mornings, the fence
Is the only silhouette
The background blankness has a chance
To symbolize. This morning's likeness
Is a jaw of pointed teeth, poised
As the baited manager strolls alongside.

IX

The Griffin at Temple Bar

THE obscene metal griffin at Temple Bar,
Spiky,
His legs pronged
Cockily apart
As if they spanned the street and all the traffic
flowed through them
As through a marble arch,
Is on a pedestal high enough to see
The private luxuries in the Law Courts windows:
The parchment light of judges' chambers,
The light shades on the ceiling, glowing delicately as
fingernails.

But the griffin's head is turned the other way.
Something's wrong here.

X

Imperial War Museum

SABRES, swords, medals, Mussolini's head,
In photographs the old-fashioned way pilots part their hair,
Victoria Crosses, dummies in gas masks,
Specimens of barbed wire, French biscuits,
Fragments of the bells of *Sermaize*,
Are faded and interesting like old books
With a monkish angle on their subjects.

Suddenly, the real sailor in uniform
Who walks between the rows of glass cases
Like any civilian Sunday visitor,
Is mummified himself.

XI

Hypnotism

I MUST write about the Tube train,
About the maps and advertisements on the walls
The black plastic straps hanging from the ceiling,
The red and green seat covers,
The matches and butts
In the trenches between the floor slats,
The complete, undiluted black
When the carriage lights go accidentally off,
I must be allowed to write about it all—
Before I become
Wrongly and willingly soothed
By the streaking tunnel colour
That waves at my speeding window.

XII

Tube Ride

THE train is waiting; I take a seat.
At the carriage window is a giant ear,
The giant paper ear, pasted on the wall outside,
Of a ruddy face that smiles and advertises beer.
It is so close I can see the coloured dots of print.
I'm used to these things. I cross my legs,
Unfold the paper and read the prickly print.
The headlines grunt at me.
My ears tuck in and fall asleep; all sounds
Are now unnoticeable as park sparrows,
The colour of the ground.

I wake up, too soon, but go on sitting comfortably,
Knowing I'm being thrown through the air
Like a speck in the hose of a vacuum cleaner.

Pipes at the window
Snaking past in the darkness
Like fossils come to life.
They pause, thin out and stretch like molten glass,
And waver like a reading on a radar screen.
They vanish. A red light ducks past the wheels.

The orange carriage air, stitched with cinders, pours
down the aisle.

My ears open and suck in dirty noises;
Chains rattle,
A gap in the track snaps at the wheels,
My bones turn to metal.

The windowpane reflects the girl's eyes opposite.
Beyond, the dark has a grain like print.
It has dots and dashes,

And pricks and tiny flashes.

A glow—the edge of a platform looms up
Like a cliff—lights—posters—notices—signs
—People of Mornington Crescent.

XIII

Discovery

NOTICE how easy it is to draw…
For sides, just a couple of upright lines,
For windows, a few quick strokes
Viciously crossing one another.
There it is, a skyscraper.

But how hard it is to draw the laced
And fruity baroque of an old West End building.

Is there any significance in this?

XIV

Lombard Street EC3

LOMBARD Street is tall and narrow,
Stone-pale, the buildings neither
Bare and modern nor old and complicated,
But pillars of a Middle Age,
They keep together in the cool.
Along the way, above the doors,
And swollen entrances
Are golden hanging things,
Trademarks, emblems, signs:
Anchor and chain,
A giant golden grasshopper,
A signboard with a cat and fiddle, too heavy to swing in the wind.
Laugh at them on their branches.
They're the freak golden apples
Of some office oracle's mythological landscape.

XV

Trafalgar Square

GANGS of pigeons stick like lice to the base
Of Nelson's Column—that comparison
Is not fair; close up they're soft and individual.
Only when I stop to think do their feet
Remind me of moon-men's wrinkled hands.

Feed them a sixpenny cup of seed.
Act naturally. The National Gallery's watching.

When I walked away and looked back
I saw that nothing mattered.
For the fountains spurted on among the people.

XVI

Suburban Illusion

THE foreign-looking turret in the English trees
Tricks whoever's interested
Into believing Russia or Turkey's at the end of the road.
Don't bother to go any farther;
It's only an emporium capped
With a borrowed bit of architecture.
The character of the women working there
Is in their spectacle frames, and the man
In charge, though polished like a sultan, is encased
In a glass ball, and when he wants to move about,
He rolls it, like a white mouse in a wheel.

XVII

Rhodesia House

BETWEEN the rows of upper windows are
crumbling headless naked statues;
There's no sign of a flag;
There used to be cut-out card board animals on
display,
But now blinds blank the ground floor windows,
And, the newspapers say,
The cut-outs have been taken away by a stranger,
To stand for something different.
A heatwave seems to burn in the building's memory;
The sun shining down into the street
Reacts on the white canvas blinds
Like the African sun that brightened pith helmets in
old colonial photographs.
On this hot day,
--The yellowed English sun lands on canvas blinds
That prove it still a bitter white,
The imperial shade on a house-paint colour-card.

XVIII

Cinema Billboard

AN oasis in the sky!
Framed in lights like a string of pearls
The giant female head
With print-golden hair, chaise-longue lips
And fanning eyelashes, above
The insect traffic. You can, for
Several silver coins, enter
The dark house below,
Where an effigy of this effigy's kept
And see her flat limbs move. Definitely
An improvement on a puppet show.
There are no pins holding her joints together.
We watched, occasionally annoyed
By a moustached man who kept coming on
Holding a smoking tommy-gun and spoiled our
view.

XVIV

Fenchurch Street Station

TRAINS from the coast pull in and their sides bleed people.
The crowds squirt through the platform gates
As if they are coming out of the sea, hurrying to get back into air.
But we are mistaken:
Their suits are dry, their hands and faces, their smiles, their hair.
To stop them now would be fatal.
Wait till each has gone down his street,
Climbed his stairs,
Opened his door
And settled
Into his chair, near his window with gilt letters.

XX

Portraits

1

THE man ahead is grateful for what he wears and carries,
A suit and a folded evening newspaper, for marking
His presence in the long blank street. In cloth-black and paper-white
They fill him in, a two-tone colour against the air.
Without them he'd be of the background, like the futile morning
Mist that hangs about the river buildings.

2

THE girl I see ahead of me,
Short skirt, shoulder-bag, her
Hair between her shoulder blades,
Is actually walking all the world at once.
There are lots of her, and if I could see
Over the building tops, I would see more
Of her. If from here I could see
Down to the coast and over the sea
To another piece of land,
And over all that, again and again,
I could appreciate her timing,

Her arms and legs swinging in step
With all the other female limbs,
A soft empire without politics or courts.

3

AN umbrella
And a *Penguin* book
Are all he needs
For confidence at night
As he gets on the bus,
Leaving behind the light
That burns for his return
Round the corner, wrinkling
In the rain.
The steel hair of his temples
Is silver as a war
Souvenir. He comes from
A house where a pipe not a gun
Smokes now, and the wall paper's
The same faraway pattern
As the look in a soldier's
Photograph on the cover
Of a fashionable history
Of the Spanish Civil War.

4

HE with clean ears, armpits
And two-tone glasses frames;
She in pearls and floral print.

Both arm and arm out to look
In the shops on a Saturday afternoon,

They pass along a brick wall,
Its hardness threatens
Their soft middle age.

It is not our fault,
Nor none of our business,
Their faces are set to say.

XXI

Tourist at the Changing of the Guard

BEFORE Buckingham Palace's black and gold railings he has come
With a thin smile on his lips
For the ceremony beyond the gravel,
That his ancestors worshipped on worn knees.
They came with a loaf of bread,
He comes with a stomach built like the mill that ground the flour,
Slung silver camera with a tinted lens,
Biting on a pipe he bought in drizzling Fleet Street in the evening edition dusk.
The guards stamp their feet and march past the windows.
The numerous teeth of his check coat laugh at them.

XXII

Approaching London from Southend

SEARCHING for the ultimate metaphor
I called to my mind a tidal beach with a fishing boat on its side.
I owed the image
To the scene beyond the track of a station
We stopped at on the way.
But the metaphor was made too late.
I tried to use it when the train
Was in a sooty junkyard sky
And running beside cabbage patches
Being hoed by old men
Who worked in the gasworks by day.

XXIII

Comforters

SOME men live to toss a bowler on a hat stand,
A pipe-stem's sterling silver ring shine,
Gossamer pinstripes, rose in the buttonhole,
Lamplight on headed notepaper.

Hear the nation sipping its tea and bunching its toes in slippers,
Rugging up is a vice, and we very much self-indulge.
Next door lives a scholar and a gentleman;
He curdles his words, bites them off by the tail
And spits them out at his guests.
The bowl of his pipe has, over the years,
Burnt away half an inch,
And his shelves are lined with books on trains.

XXIV

Colour Supplement

YOU'RE fond of colours, madam?
A standing egg yolk really turns you on?
Don't bother to go to Africa for ochre,
That hue which warms your sodden eyes.
Now you can have it in the privacy of your living-
room.
Like cheese at no extra cost
The supplement lies sandwiched in a folded
newspaper.

Advertisements for brilliantine and sherry
Will light up and dry out your living-room
And distract you from the city greys
Grizzling at the window.

XXV

Waterloo Station: Morning

IN some back room,
Shut off from shoe
Shuffling and noise
Of change at ticket windows,
A tape's unwinding quietly
From a spool.
It sends a stream
Of music through
The ears of crowds
Then up to pigeons
On the girders.
Powerful things
Work quietly—
The heart, an atom
Waiting to be split.
The music seeps
Like green gas through
The porous crowds.
Its purpose is
To kill off thoughts
Of two world wars.

Give every step
Of every shiny
Shoe and pinstripe
Trouser leg the grandeur
Of a Broadway musical.

The way out’s down some steps.
Above, a war memorial,
Like plaster ceiling fruit,
Sooty and unnoticed.

Out in the street,
The taxis of the air run you down.

XXVI

Drug Addict on The Strand

SITTING beside an Underground entrance,
Grinning inwardly like an actor,
Into the darkened audience of my greatcoat,
I feel strong enough to read the small print on a distant news stand.

On the way here I passed a cinema;
I stopped and stepped into the stills stuck up outside:
Two men were fighting on the ground;
I led the girl looking on as far as the white photographic border.

I've given my body up to its own means,
And stand by,
Curious of what it might do.

It realises that what tastes so delicious
Is the other end of itself.
A chemical reaction's better than a physical one,

And after what has mixed with my blood,
I’ve taught myself
To take the very life out of a pebble,
Just by staring at it.

XXVII

Lunchtimes

1
DOWN a bigoted alley
Between great streets,
I peel golden foil
Off chocolate drops, struggling
With bitten fingernails
To grip an edge.
My shirt is yesterday's,
And the crumbs of last night's sleep
Are still in the corners of my eyes.
My teeth already ache with sweetness.

2
WARM I stepped from a bath of bar air.
I had leant on polished oak,
And horse brass on the mantelpiece had shined at me.
My fingers were yellow with lager light.
In the flats of the street now I am.
Among buildings and beyond them
A zoo of landmarks and monuments lie in wait for me.

XXVIII

Pensioner on an Autumn Sunday Night

I DON'T know what it is,
But something in this Sunday night reminds me of the War.
Something big feels to be approaching.
The air is pulled across like black-out curtains,
And in my head there flashes on and off a picture of distant civilians digging.

Now I remember. I remember
The wireless crackling,
Big Ben's solemn dong,
The warbling of Neville Chamberlain's phlegm, breath whistling through his teeth.

For a minute I thought that lorry going by
Was coming from the sky.

• * *

He went to bed and dreamed
Of loose bricks the wind blew about like snow.

FOR ST VALENTINE'S DAY

IT'S more than five years since we met
But seems five days are not up yet,
So strong a current flows through us.
We glow, and moth-friends come to view us.
We celebrate just like the young.
We're dripping ardour still, not wrung
By busy poets saying all
True love must die or fall
In fruitful yet in downward curve
Slowly to kill passion's sealed nerve,
As in good teeth no longer cleaned.
Let poets be demeaned
By our example. Are we smug?
Perhaps we are, and simply chug,
Not soar. But I know flight
When I feel it; I must be right:
For we will go a greater height yet;
The alp top's not in sight yet
And might never be in our lifetime.

1977

TWO YEARS AFTER MY MOTHER’S DEATH

(i)

MY mind is in a state of shocked applause,
My only explanation: ‘It’s a trick!’
Out by what trapdoor, panel, or slung gauze
Did my dead mother flick?

She must be somewhere—out of sight, around
A corner, on a trip; I grope
For the hole she’s disappeared down.
My brain’s a pen that’s nibbled by a schoolboy dope.

(ii)

Plain and simple as a pinafore,
Death seemed too important for her lore,
And pain distinguished her much more.
Jungle and living-room are the same
In the end. From the ornament shelf came
A tiger among glass-blown animals.
It grew to life-size, watched by cannibals;
It mauled her for a year and she died
The slow death of a mouse.

(iii)

I was a well-seated spectator, packed
Stalls to her coming to pieces, I,
Prime carcass offensively intact,
I wanted to punish myself and die
In sympathy, by going with her, taut
Like a journalist—and come back to report.

(iv)

Was she seized and taken, or did she go
Willingly?—She, so particular that I
Should wrap up and keep warm against the snow,
Slid off a foggy drop not thinking why,
Leaving her body behind, an overcoat.

(v)

Spontaneous combustion has full smoked
Her up, but I disregard the process;
I see death a street accident provoked
To have me gently lay the poultice press
On the swelling hurt. This is the end, preacher;
The book's last page turned, and the final task
Has been completed, and sorry, teacher,
Whoever you are—I cannot grasp
The lesson.
1977

THE NOISE AND THE LOOK

A FAMOUS man who snuffs his thoughts
And creeps outside at night to thrill
At all who wander through his courts
To glimpse him as event of sports
Feels like a statue on a hill.

When I step out the slope is bare;
All scenes I prop up soon fall flat;
Always a noise but nothing there.
I am resigned to sit and stare
With my wife and my marmalade cat.

Who'll face the fact his tale's been told?
I cannot face it; for the look
Of telling longing to unfold
Stands out on every face like old
Print in a classic story book.

BATHROOM SOLO

O HOW I want to stay
In this hot bath today!
The whole day I'll stay
To keep the cold away.

I wear liquid bedclothes
And quilt, spread from my nose,
Without pucker or tuck,
To my white wrinkled toes.

I know this water cover
Won't stay warm forever,
And I'll be twice as iced
When I at last leave here.

But when I hear the squall
Of hailstones through the wall
I've not, I tell you, got
The sense to act at all.

30 January 1969

A SEASIDE ACCIDENT

MY little dog that quickly died
Had tried to reach the beach across
The empty friendly esplanade,
The road that runs with sea beside,
Empty, deadly: for came the gross
And metal beast that knocked her hard.

Dead artist now with broken flair,
Did she insist too much clear ground
In swallowing that vast air
Of sea and sky; did she demand
Free passage for the leap and bound
As dusk breeze praised the perfect sand?

She thought as does the tiny sprat
Which darts across the tidal pool
That once alive is always that,
Though she will get, like I get mine,
The sudden sideways nudge to fool
The beautifully ruled straight line.

I must not blame the ignorant
And innocent blood droplet there,
Blind to the motor and its slant;
The trusted hand laid chance's bait
On that last day of broken care
With careless, waiting, open gate.

Grange beach, 1960

LEFT ALONE

YOU left me alone only this minute,
Catch-click and door-slam still
Sound in my head:
I thought no time had passed,
But, oh, instead,
The house grows strange as if you'd never lived in it.

The light globes burn on, never having known,
The fridge chugs through the silence
Left by you,
Says, 'I only know I've got
A job to do.'
I jolt at the fact that you've left me alone

On this lonely public holiday afternoon.
The tree at the window
Rings with birds,
Our cat returns along
The fence tops—words
Come, but must go wasted, for I'm alone.

Your touch made home for me from just a stack
Of landlord's furniture,

But now you're elsewhere,
The strangeness spreads: I taste
What I must bear
Full strength the day you go and can't come back.

TO US

OUR dearest memories are match-flare small:
Dark room rent peace with snapshot glare shut out,
And holiday-numb strolls through towns where all
Are strangers, where at last we're free to shout
At least we're puzzle parts that click, like pence,
Side by side in the giant thudding
Jigsaw that paves all ways…These moments
Are earthworks made beautiful by flooding.

But we submerge too much. My rising pride
Is stricken with the bends. Doomed flesh-cast
show—
My diving memory's bloodstream bubbles hide
Tableaux of our censored scenes, to stud
The heart. Events, please silt our moat and grotto
Stealth until we're relic calm on farmyard mud.

THE ICE BROKE AND WE DROWNED

Three deaths on a Hampstead Pond.
The footprints on the ice remained for days

GOOD solid life stood all around,
The day's dull furniture on view;
What we expected was what we found—
We threw a ball and the ball bounced true.

Everything was what it seemed
(Stupidity was our ale);
We trod the ice, the ice gleamed,
Life's exam we were about to fail.

Alive was all we'd ever been.
We swung on the world, and the branch held.
Then dusk—ice—a picture scene.
We danced, the spell broke, time yelled.

1970s?

THE TRIAL SEPARATION

'DON'T see me for a while,' you say.
Our words can only trip and bump:
Our feelings hurt, torn, in the way,
Are bitten nails that scratch the rump.

We burn apart, I am divorced,
A glowing, whitish stump, a thumb
Without a classic, which is forced
To flick mere pages you've become—

The light behind your blind at night
Is all of you I can expect;
And in the street, though in full sight,
Distance turns you to an insect.

Bickering's dangerous drug,
Destroys the cells of love, eats through
Our tapestry of living rug
So that a foreign land sleets through.

Events perform a masque for me,
Mistakes can be rewritten;
My role's a ghost no one can see,
Yet who can touch and has been bitten.

Tissue can repair itself,
Mistakes become, like junk, antiques;
Love that was put high on the shelf
Is stirred, unclots, and warms our cheeks.

1977

GREAT OPENINGS FOR A MARMALADE CAT

Though a blizzard blows in the bedroom
And our toes are snapping off,
And what sounds like someone sawing
Is the rasping of our cough—
What of that?
I must leave the window open for my marmalade cat.

The rain's put out the heater,
The teapots blocked with snow,
There's a waiting-list for burglars,
The walls are wet—I know.
Too bad, that.
All things that shut *stay open* for my marmalade cat.

What's that sound of glassware smashing,
And that clawing of the rug?
What's that sound of curtains slashing,
Who broke the Toby jug?
What's that sound of china crashing,
That splash of boiling fat?—
The complete run of the house he has—my magnificent marmalade cat.

Come in, sit down, don't be a grouch,

Though the furniture's not the best:
The back is torn out of the couch,
There's not even one chair for a guest.
So whether your culture is East,
Of whether your culture is West,
You must sit on the floor and eat off the door
Till the cat's had his food and rest.

TO MY LOVE

I WAS a quail-mind struggling in the grass:
Better to flutter in the tangled weeds
Than risk in open sky more fallen deeds.
You swept the clutter, cut a mountain pass,
Gave me solid floor to act my farce.
Persistent builder you on marshy meads
Where men you chose have sunk at varying speeds,
But we two rise, twin bubbles in a glass.

The clothes of romance that hang bright on sale
Are not to style our love, we do not fit;
We have no marriage in the fairy tale
Of social fabric; we ourselves must knit
Our own philosophy and drive the nail
To fix a creed for when the cannon hit.

1986

DO-IT-YOURSELF VALENTINE

INSTEAD of a card with a velvet heart
I’ve thought of a poem and sent you the start.

FORGOTTEN FLOWERS

THE flowers that dress our wedding aisle impress
As cups of a kind:
They hold the marriage moment more or less,
Bowls left behind
To beg a purpose from the carven emptiness.

The guests have gone. The softness cleverly built
Is too long after
Cradled by bride and groom, now dressed in guilt,
Returned from laughter:
Carnations, dahlias, stocks, about to wilt.

Stood in buckets, saved from a cruel elsewhere,
Drinking at last,
Martyrs at water behind our house here
Break their fast;
At sun are forgotten flowers of this remembered
year.

A PRIVILEGED VIEW OF MEMORIES FROM THE KITCHEN COUNTER

I stand and do not stir,
No victim of crime,
No political unrest,
No illness or time,
To put me to the test,
I stand and do not stir:
I am a lucky voyeur.

Here come the memories,
They float, ah, float, then flow;
Old structures have collapsed
I sift among the mow;
And shy smears paste scenes splashed
Driving past: streams that minds freeze,
A quilt across the knees.

Some memories are thin,
In tanks that stand in time's
Old measures: with my held,
Pointed love I prise,
And lever minutes from old,
Reserved hours set within
A stored day, and I captain—
The sailing picture panes:

People, animals, herd
And plants, all far behind
The eyes: they come forward,
Hung along the mind,
The long remembrance hall.
Lone leaves, out of the wall
On running river ploy,
Settle a few ticks,
Soaked colours, dim edge skimming,
Seep, then slow moved mix--
West Beach, my Father swimming
Underwater, a boy
On his back clinging, coy;
Shy sea floor crabs that nipped
And disappeared in sand;
Old beach radio wave,
Shark reports; backyard ants
I stepped aside to save,
My dog or cat gazing, gripped,
By that which distance clipped.
Innocent human talk,
Speech from beloved shape
Of mouths forever closed.
After dark, sea hissing to the cape,
Night on the esplanade posed
By little clouds of fawn
Sand the wind puffed to stalk.

Memories are income,
Unearned income but paid,
And no illness splinter,
Nor those whom death squads slayed.
Free at kitchen counter
No political unrest
To put me to the test.
I stand and do not stir
I am a privileged voyeur.

I do not suffer yet
Because I do not wander
Outside, but I ponder
At the kitchen counter.
I'm a lucky *flaneur*
I'm a privileged voyeur.
I stand and do not stir.

IN MEMORY OF HELEN McCRORY

died 16 April 2021

We, the performers.
This time you were in an audience,
my audience. You came to me after my show.
Your face displaced the air of end,
and apple presence hung above the windfalls,
my folding table of spent tricks,
the open suitcase with a lolling puppet rabbit,
deprived of life till next show.

I had seen you in a man-and-woman head-and-
shoulders drama on my screen at home, and I
imagined people's screens with you on them in
many houses.

I had done something in a similar way with comedy.
I hadn't thought you knew all my trophy cups
engraved, my hidden-camera pranks on people's
screens.
You—content with this, my tiny children's show
beyond the exercise machines and the heated pool
one sacred Sunday morning,
in a health club planted near London, at one end of a
borrowed room,
children rapt or not, mothers, fathers, nannies

watching or not, one woman boldly ignoring and reading.

Why you were in the audience I never knew or asked.

Two waged pretenders
that morning,
resting on the images we made
to please the public.

You praised my other art beyond that room and screen,
my Tube Theatre on the platforms
and in the carriages of the London Underground,
since that health club morning you have become a name to a face,
and I, who was almost a name to a face, stayed at a face and faded.

The day you stopped being available for life,
our face-to-face became a memory
in just my mind —unless you…unless there is…
Thank you for that, Helen, for your walk to my end of the room.

THE SEA-WATER SWIMMING POOL

A cuboid of sea sucked, a measured, a metred cut,
still and smooth,
and sunk smug beside the shifting
rearing plains
of St Vincent Gulf, donor
of this sea-mock block
which tries to better the sea.
This bound salt-water prisoner
flattens
behind walls of mesh-wire
stretched with canvas,
to hide the sea blows, the
Portuguese man-o-wars,
porpoises, and sharks.
We trod the edge on duckboards damp or dry,
on the tiled, slippery aisles that
shone long
with seawater slithering off us:
we childhoods returning with our
whipping towels to the
changing rooms.

Swimmers driving backstroke
along the pool,

between corked lanes, the tiled
finish in sight—
backstroke, breaststroke, freestyle,
butterfly!
Arms pierced the gloss,
bodies creeping along,
and feet beat boils of foam.

The tiles, home tiles at last we
touched to end
a race or training session, and
panting,
to get our breath back.

The pool was emptied for cleaning,
then refilled on loan from the
waters beyond.
But one day it was emptied of
sea—
and filled with earth,
Filled in.
Concrete is there now—parking
spaces.
The sea never noticed.

Henley Pool 1934-85

SEAFRONT MEMORY

BRUSHING of the sun, the salt air;
Sometimes the storm-borne spume
Worried painted window frames bare,
Outside the lenient walls, my room.

Above, hung rampart emptiness:
Remembered blue, few small clouds grazed.
Below, the suspect sea, depth guessed,
Then beach, whose solid floor tides glazed.

The jutting jetty's crossbeams stitched
A stretched sea, coaxed and called me
To walk on water. Not locked, but latched,
Were lenient limits then that walled me.

Grange circa 1965

TO THE MARTYRS OF THE DOG-MEAT TRADE

BACK STREET sheds, yards, red wet filthy stone floors.

Even yet tail-wagging in an opened cage
until giant iron tongs
close and pull you out by the neck, someone's stolen pet,
to hurt you to the reverse of mercy.

Deepest shaft of pain sunk in you
the longest time but without
letting you die, till death insists,
done to make they say the tastiest dinner;
tourists laughing, photographing.

You martyrs, taught to love your enemies, never forgive us.

IN MEMORY OF THE DUKE OF EDINBURGH

died 9 April 2021

MERLEAU-PONTY'S phenomenology
Says whenever I open my eyes to see
The world, it's all my own work. From childhood on,
Newsreel, and newspaper, and news good on

TV, from horizon to heaven you
Came and went and came like a building who
From a car window on life's outings showed
Again at last, with a turn of the road.

You neared with astonishing clarity
Among the small groups holding cups of tea
At St James's Palace where I was sent
For a world war centenary event

In memory of my soldier grandfather.
A walking image came across the floor, rather
As if freed from a newspaper's pages,
Or films I had seen throughout my ages

Had let you go on leave. You asked me what

My relative did. I said he was not
In the first landings, but he went ashore
A later wave, a soldier delayed what's more

By the good or bad luck of having bad
Teeth. 'What's that?' I can quote you having said,
'He didn't have to bite the enemy,
Did he!' People pretend that royalty,

Is definitely a job they would turn down.
You proved it could be done with more than gown,
Smile and wave, And could be done with the Queen
As straight man, being serious in between.

WINDOWS

*Everything unknown is taken as marvellous; but now the limits of Britain
are laid bare.—Tacitus, c. 55-117 AD, from* Agricola

DON'T believe a lit window's trick of light,
Award not your own sun behind that glass,
Expect no achievement like the bird's flight.

Don't believe crossing seas for a great right
Would land you rich in a great city's mass,
Don't believe a lit window's trick of light.

Though windows grow on high in promised sight,
Do not stretch upwards from your narrow pass,
Expect no achievement like the bird's flight.

Do not think the one behind the glass might
Give you a trumpet to play in love's brass,
Don't believe a lit window's trick of light.

Do not believe dead genius is quite
You in another life or in fame's class:
Expect no achievement like the bird's flight.

The lighted window in the dark is bright
Not for you; cease the body double farce.
Don't believe a lit window's trick of light,
Expect no achievement like the bird's flight.

INDEX OF *TITLES* AND FIRST LINES

TUBE TH

www.ingramcontent.com/pod-product-compliance
Lightning Source LLC
Chambersburg PA
CBHW060623310726
48982CB00003B/655

* 9 7 8 1 7 3 9 8 4 1 4 0 9 *